# Fairy Tale Theater
# SNOW WHITE AND THE SEVEN DWARFS

Illustrations by: CARME PERIS
Adapted by: MÓNICA BOSOM

## CHARACTERS:
Snow White, the Queen, the Mirror, the Hunter, the Seven Dwarfs, the Prince, the Forest Animals

**Narrator:**

Once upon a time there was a Queen who had a little girl as white as snow, with lips as red as blood and hair as dark as coal. She called her Snow White. When the little girl was born, the Queen died and her father married again, this time a woman who was as beautiful as she was vain and cruel and who owned a magic mirror, to which she always asked the same question:

**Queen:** *(Addressing the magic mirror)*
*"Mirror, mirror, on the wall,*
*Who in this kingdom is the fairest of all?"*

**Mirror:**

*"You, my Queen, you are the fairest of all!"*

**Narrator:**

The Queen asks the mirror the same question day after day and she does not realize that Snow White has grown prettier every day.

**Queen:**

  *"Mirror, mirror, on the wall,*
  *Who in this kingdom is the fairest of all?"*

**Mirror:**

  *"Oh, my Queen, what I am saying is true.*
  *Snow White is more beautiful than you."*

**Queen:** *(She goes green with envy and red with anger. She calls a hunter to her.)*

  "Take Snow White into the forest and kill her. I want you to bring me her cloak as proof."

**Hunter:** *(Takes out a knife)*

  "Snow White, we are already in the forest and I must obey the Queen."

**Snow White:** *(Crying)*

  "Please do not kill me! I promise you never to return to the palace!"

**Hunter:** *(Feeling sorry for her)*

"Give me your cloak and run away. I will stain the cloak with rabbit blood and the Queen will never know I have disobeyed her. *(Talking to himself)* Anyway, it will not be long before the wild animals devour poor Snow White."

**Snow White:**

"It is getting dark. I am hungry, cold, and afraid. These trees look bigger than usual and these animals do not look very friendly. I am tired of running and tripping over roots. But ... what is that? It is a small house, right in front of me. *(She goes in.)* Oh, what a pretty little house! Everything is in order and the table is set *(she counts)* with seven small plates, seven knives, seven forks, and seven little glasses. I will eat a little from each plate, so it will not show. *(Looking to the side)* Mmmmm ... I am sleepy! There are seven little beds here, but they are so small I can only fit in the last one."

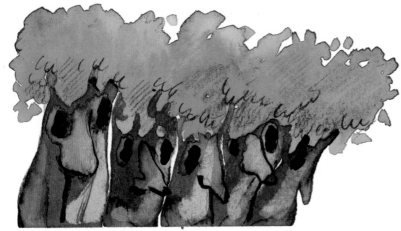

**Narrator:**

Snow White falls asleep and at midnight there arrive seven dwarfs, home from their work in the mines in the mountains.

**First Dwarf:**

"Who has sat in my little chair?"

**Second Dwarf:**

"Who has eaten from my little plate?"

**Third Dwarf:**

"Who has tasted my little bread?"

**Fourth Dwarf:**

"Who has used my little fork?"

**Fifth Dwarf:**

"Who has eaten my vegetables?"

**Sixth Dwarf:**

"Who has cut with my little knife?"

**Seventh Dwarf:**

"Who has drunk from my little glass?"

**First Dwarf:**

"Someone has used my bed."

**Dwarfs:**

"And mine? And mine?"

**Narrator:**

They all run from bed to bed, until in the last one ...

**Seventh Dwarf** (*Discovering Snow White*)

"It is a girl, and she is so pretty!"

**Snow White:** (*She wakes up and is frightened.*)

"Who are you?"

**Dwarfs:**

"What is your name, and how did you get here?"

**Snow White:**

"My name is Snow White and I have run away from my wicked stepmother because she wanted to kill me."

**Dwarfs:**

"Then stay with us, but be careful, because if your stepmother hears you are alive, she will try again to kill you. Most of all, do not open the door to anyone."

**Narrator:**
And that is how Snow White stayed to live with the dwarfs and cook for them and clean their cottage.

*(At the Queen's palace)*

**Queen:** *(The Queen questions the mirror.)*
*"Mirror, mirror, on the wall,*
*Who in this kingdom is the fairest of all?"*

**Mirror:**
*"You, my Queen, are the one I see*
*but at the house of the Seven Dwarfs*
*lives Snow White,*
*and none is so fair as she!"*

**Queen:**
"That is not possible! The hunter has fooled me and Snow White is still alive. But she will not have her way. I will poison an apple but it will look so appetizing that Snow White will not be able to resist biting it. I will dress like an old lady and will go to the house of the Seven Dwarfs. It will be easy to fool Snow White."

**Old Lady:** *(She knocks on the door at the house of the Seven Dwarfs.)*

Knock, knock, knock!

**Snow White:**

"Who is knocking? What do you want? I cannot let anyone in."

**Old Lady:**

"I am just an old lady who has come to offer you an apple." *(Takes the appetizing-looking apple from her basket)*

**Snow White:**

"No, thank you. I cannot accept it."

**Old Lady:**

"Are you afraid it is poisoned? I will split it in two and we will both eat a half."

**Narrator:**

The old lady eats the half that was not poisoned and Snow White eats the other half. As soon as Snow White bites the apple, she falls to the floor. Meanwhile, the old lady has transformed herself again into the Queen and is back at her palace.

**Queen:** *(In one of the rooms of the palace)*
*"Mirror, mirror, on the wall,*
*Who in all this kingdom is the fairest of all?"*

**Mirror:**

*"You, my Queen, you are the fairest of all!"*

**Narrator:**

That day the dwarfs get home at the usual time. They find Snow White lying on the floor and no breath coming out of her mouth. She is dead. They try to bring her back to life but the beautiful Snow White is no longer alive.

**First Dwarf:**

"She is dead! Her stepmother has poisoned her with this apple. Look, she still has some of it in her hand."

**Second Dwarf:**

"We will make her a glass coffin and we will mourn her in the middle of the forest."

**Narrator:**

All the dwarfs agree. They place the coffin in the middle of the forest and the dwarfs and the forest animals mourn the beautiful Princess. One day, a Prince passes by.

**Prince:** *(Moved)*

"She is so pretty, I will not be able to live without looking at her. Please let me take the coffin to my palace."

**Dwarfs:**

"As you seem to have a kind heart, you can take Snow White with you."

**Narrator:**

The servants of the Prince carry the coffin and walk and walk, and suddenly, they trip on some bushes. With the shock of the fall, Snow White coughs up the little piece of poisoned apple she had swallowed.

**Snow White:** *(Waking up)*

"Where am I? What has happened to me?"

**Prince:** *(Full of joy)*

"Oh, you are alive! I am so happy! I love you more than anything in the world and I want you to be my wife."

**Snow White:** *(Happily)*

"Yes, I want to be your wife."

*(Meanwhile, at the palace)*

**Queen:**

"Mirror, mirror, on the wall,
Who in this kingdom is the fairest of all?"

**Mirror:**

"Oh, my Queen, what I am saying is true.
Snow White is more beautiful than you."

**Narrator:**

The Queen smashes the mirror in rage. Snow White and the Prince celebrate their marriage with great joy and splendor. The evil Queen becomes so sick with envy and rage, that she finally dies.

# ACTIVITIES

Some of the activities related to this play can include:

1.  Children can make an imaginary playground or neighborhood using colored pencils and construction paper. They can draw houses, lakes, swings, sandboxes, fountains, and other things found in a playground or neighborhood.

2. Make a toy house from recycled objects. Use a cardboard box to form the frame of the house. For furniture, children can use empty matchboxes, cardboard tubes, toothpicks, and thread bobbins. Windows and doors can be cut out. Children can make curtains out of paper and then glue or staple them in place.

3. Play the apple bite game. Attach the two ends of a length of string to two opposite walls. Hang apples on the string, at various heights, by tying different lengths of string to the stem of each apple. Children then must try to bite the apples without using their hands.

4. Another activity consists of making very simple finger puppets. Cut out each character shown in the illustration and paste onto cardboard. Make the two cuts indicated in the drawing.

Place the puppets on your fingers and act out the story.

--- cut
--- cut

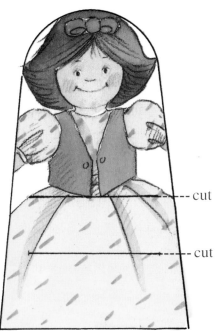
--- cut
--- cut

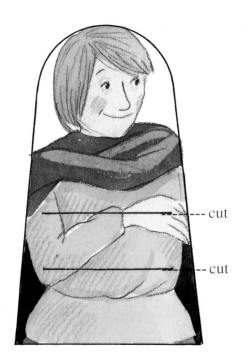
--- cut
--- cut

--- cut
--- cut

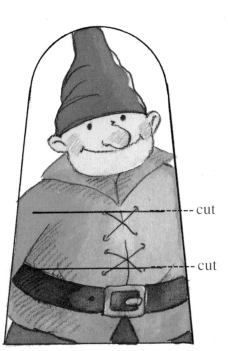
--- cut
--- cut

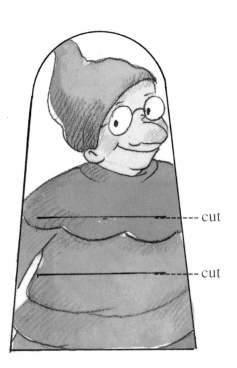
--- cut
--- cut

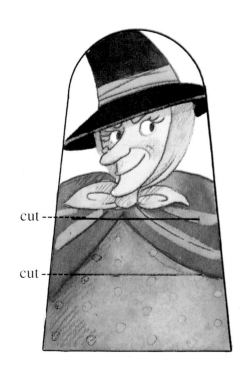

cut -------

cut -------

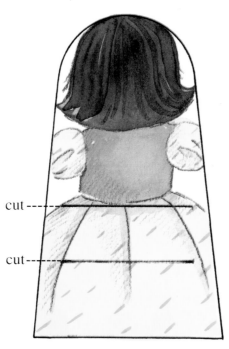

cut -------

cut -------

cut -------

cut -------

cut -------

cut -------

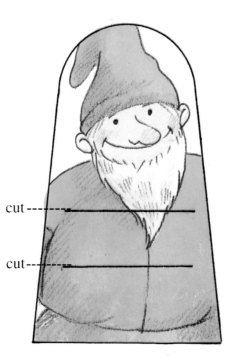

cut -------

cut -------

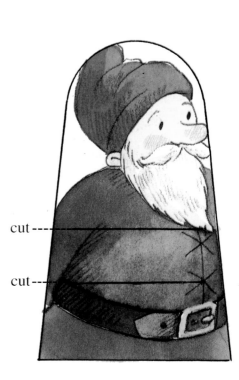

cut -------

cut -------

English language version published by Barron's Educational Series, Inc., 1999

Original title of the book in Catalan:
BLANCANEUS I ELS SET NANS
One in the series *Teatre dels contes*
Illustrations by Carme Peris
Adapted by Mónica Bosom
Design by Carme Peris

Copyright © TREVOL PRODUCCIONS EDITORIALS, S.C.P., 1999. Barcelona, Spain.

*All inquiries should be addressed to:*
Barron's Educational Series, Inc.
250 Wireless Boulevard
Hauppauge, New York 11788
http://www.barronseduc.com

International Standard Book No. 0-7641-5151-7

*Library of Congress Catalog Card No. 98-73631*

Printed in Spain
9 8 7 6 5 4 3 2 1